Contents

Introduction

Where will families eat tonight?

Perhaps they will go out to eat at a favorite chain restaurant or local diner. Maybe they're visiting Grandma at her assisted-living facility and joining her for supper there. There might be a special occasion tonight that calls for something formal and upscale. Perhaps they're on a cruise or staying in a hotel with room service. Or maybe there's only time to pick up a family value pack from the drive-through window. They might swing by the supermarket and pick up some prepared foods along with the week's groceries. Wherever they go, there will be a meal waiting for them. And each meal is also a career opportunity. Because everybody's got to eat. So that means someone has to do the cooking.

Being a cook means long hours, disciplined behavior, and hard work, but it also means steady paychecks and a set of skills that translate across so many different kitchens. It's easy to think of cooking or serving food as a career as work that's strictly for fancy restaurants with snooty waiters and snootier customers or as flipping burgers at a fast-food chain. But in actuality, professional kitchens exist in many, many places and forms. From diners to Chipotle to hotels and cruise ships to catering to nursing homes, where there are people gathered together, they will want to be fed.

This is a guide for those who want to be the backbone of the kitchen, who want to be able to find work wherever they go, and who may even want a little creativity in their jobs. It's easy to think of a restaurant

Eating a meal together is a great way to connect with one another, no matter who did the cooking.

career as something between the extremes of fine dining or fast-food chains, but there are so many different opportunities out there for professional cooks and chefs beyond fancy establishments. There are also opportunities in the front of the house, where wait staff can rise up to general managers and other leadership roles that require organization and interaction with customers. Cooks and other restaurant staff may start at the bottom of the hierarchy, but each step up will bring new skills to prepare them for their greater responsibilities. A life in the world of prepared food will bring tight relationships, cooperation under pressure, and the satisfaction of a hard job done night after night, day after day.

CHAPTER One

Life on the Line

The restaurant kitchen is where the training for a life "on the line" will usually begin. It's also the place where the vocabulary and hierarchy of the kitchen are taught. Anyone interested in a culinary career should learn the common terms used by professional

Cooks all work together "on the line" to fill a table's orders. Sometimes, one dish can be put together by multiple people throughout the kitchen!

cooks. Fine dining will have more ranks and specialized terminology than a short-order cook at a diner or a fast-casual place like Chipotle, but there's still a common language and chain of command throughout all kitchens.

Feel the Heat

The professional kitchen is methodical and organized regardless of any fine dining credentials. The head of the command is the executive chef, the *chef de cuisine*, or the head cook. Next in line is always the right-hand cook, the *sous-chef*, who is like the vice president to the head chef's presidential rank in the kitchen. Truly fine dining has an army of cooks, according to the classic French method of organizing and running a kitchen, and it can be intimidating navigating each station—a place in the kitchen with a specific job assigned to it. However, before any newbies ever pick up a knife, they will start at the simplest place of all: the kitchen sink.

Zach Benson got his start in short-order and fast-casual places before moving on to catering and institutional kitchens. In every place though, he says, "Basic kitchen duties normally always start in the dish pit. Then you work your way to basic prep, which doesn't involve much cooking, just chopping, peeling, etc." Jordan Arnold has been a line cook in high-end restaurants as well as more casual places, and though he now works in the front of the house, he agrees. "I got [a dishwashing] gig from the local classified section, at fourteen. It was pretty simple work for a local restaurant: clock in, wash from the lunch rush, set up for dinner,

Prep work is the foundation of all restaurant cooking. Without the ingredients precut and ready, it's really easy for cooks to fall "in the weeds."

finish with a sweep and mop." It seems weird being paid for what is essentially a household chore, but the skills are crucial to a longer career in the kitchen. Arnold found it very useful for his later cooking years. What these tasks teach are how time is managed in the kitchens—when they'll be busy, and what needs to be prioritized sooner than later.

Once the dishwashing has been mastered, and the people in charge know a person's serious about moving up in the kitchen, the next step is prep work. This still won't be cooking with heat or assembling dishes, but it's one of the most essential roles in the kitchen. Every vegetable peeled, chopped, or diced is a key ingredient in a cook's *mise-en-place*, meaning "everything in place." It's French, and it means everything is all set up for the cooks to execute their dishes properly. Dishwashers may find themselves helping with the larger, more monotonous prep tasks, like removing strings from snow peas, or cutting up all the vegetables needed for roasting.

MASTERING THE ART OF THE FRENCH KITCHEN

David Kamp's book *The United States of Arugula* details the evolution of good food and fine dining in the United States, where he tracks the various influences that have led to the contemporary New American style of food often found in finer restaurants today. However, the organization of the professional kitchen is attributed to the French, who have a regimented system with ranks. Below is the basic hierarchy of roles and responsibilities in the classic French workplace:

Chef de cuisine: The head chef who plans the meals and oversees the kitchen.
Sous-chef: Directly runs the kitchen and is the right-hand associate for the chef de cuisine.
Chefs de partie: Chefs in charge of a particular preparation in a restaurant kitchen. These include:

- ***Saucier:*** In charge of stocks, sauces, and sautéing meat.
- ***Entremetier:*** The vegetable cook who also is in charge of soups and omelets.
- ***Poissonier:*** The fish cook.
- ***Rôtissier:*** The roast cook, who handles the heavier cooking of meats like broiling and roasting, as well as fried foods.
- ***Garde-manger:*** In charge of cold dishes like pâtés.
- **Pâtissier:** The pastry chef, who is in charge of desserts.
- ***Boucher:*** The butcher.
- ***Chef de tournant:*** The chef who can jump in on any station and help out.

Commis: The cooks who work under the chefs de partie and who can be ranked by seniority. An especially large kitchen might see as many as six commis to one department.

Beyond prep work comes the actual cooking. No matter what kind of kitchen it is, Benson and Arnold both agree that the next step up the food chain is the garde-manger station, which is responsible for salads and cold foods such as sandwiches. Or perhaps the fryer station might be the place where a cook is welcomed to the line. The more complicated cooking of meat and main entrées is reserved for the most experienced cooks. There can be overlap between duties or doubling up of responsibilities, but no matter the type of kitchen, it's reasonable to assume the hierarchy is arranged by dishes, then prep, then cold foods, and last of all, hot foods. So, first comes basic prep work. Once that's been mastered, one can move into first the basic recipes, then more complicated ones. The chain of command gets moved up too as a cook advances through the line. The first step is running one crew, then all the crews, as one becomes the sous, who answers to the head chef.

Training and Prep

Before entering a professional kitchen as a career path, it's wise to learn some basic food vocabulary and techniques. Much of the language and standard culinary methods are derived from the classic French kitchens and cooks. The renowned French chef Jacques Pépin wrote *La Technique* in 1974 as a way to demystify the fundamentals of French cooking to nonprofessional cooks. Over forty years later, it's still in print and helping cooks at every level to understand the language of food preparation, including the most basic skills, like how to hold a knife properly. A revised edition came out in 2012 and is available at many libraries. "Just as in 1974," Pépin writes, "the greatest hindrance to good performance knowledge is basic cooking techniques." That's why the very first food prep he teaches is with the most basic and fundamental ingredient in pretty much all cuisines and is done with the most important tool a cook can own—that is, how to properly chop an onion. Mastering that technique with that ingredient is the core of all cooking and can be practiced at any time. "When professionals work with ease and rapidity, it is a result of long years of practice and discipline," says Pépin. "There are no secrets or tricks, only feats of skill…acquired with prolonged effort." In other words, practice really does make perfect.

However, it's not just understanding the actual tools and methods that a professional cook needs to know. One should understand that it's a fast-moving workplace requiring the ability to stay focused no matter how hot or loud the kitchen is or how the orders are coming in. The US Bureau of Labor Statistics notes that the hours are long and often start very early in the morning or running until very late at night. The hours will also include working on weekends and holidays, the prime times for people to be out and dining, which can be a strain on family time, or a blessing for those who want to escape it.

Perhaps the biggest factor separating professional cooks from home ones is consistency. Fine dining is much more detail-oriented. If one pumps out fifty salads in a day, all those plates better look and taste exactly the same. That consistency takes a lot of effort and a lot of mistakes along the way, to be honest. In professional cooking, it's hard work every day, and one gets instant feedback on whether the cooking succeeded and failed. A good cook needs speediness, knife skills, and cleanliness. But a long-lasting cook also needs focus, a sense of humor, and a thick skin.

THE COOKING BASICS

According to Jacques Pépin in *La Technique*, there are some standard techniques and ingredients a professional kitchen worker may be expected to understand:

Chop (also "dice" and "mince"): Cutting the ingredients into small pieces. A fine dining restaurant cares deeply about the details, so precision is very important, especially when making the pieces uniform. Perhaps smaller pieces will be needed, which is known as a *dice* or in French, as a *brunoise*, which is a very fine dice that's also very uniform and even. Mince is the smallest cut of all, and is often used for products like garlic in order to spread a flavorful ingredient throughout the dish without overwhelming the other components.

Component: The ingredients of a dish, but also how the dish is broken down into different sections. A steak is one component, its sauce is another, and the buttered peas on the side are a third component.
Brown: Cooking a piece of meat on all sides until it's brown all the way around. Usually, this is done before a long cooking time in a crockpot or oven.
Boil: Heating up liquid quickly over high heat until it's bubbling rapidly.

(continued on the next page)

Having an understanding of the basic techniques and terms used in the kitchen helps young cooks advance through the ranks.

(continued from the previous page)

Simmer: Heating up liquid at a slow pace and low temperature until it's just under the boiling point.
Poach: Cooking a protein or hearty vegetable in simmering liquid.
Sear: This technique is much like browning, but it's done at a higher heat, often for shorter times than browning. A sear can add great taste and a lot of texture to a dish.
Sauté: Cooking something in oil or cooking fat over lower heats and stirring the ingredients regularly.
Fry: Cooking something in oil or cooking fat over high heat. Stirring keeps the ingredients from sticking to the pan.
Reduce: Cooking liquids for a long time, often over high heats in order to shrink the amount of liquid in the pot. The thicker consistency and depth of flavor will be even stronger in the soups and sauces than in simmering.
Protein: The base of the entrée, more or less. This term covers meats, poultry, fish, and vegetarian options like tofu or beans. Most menus design their dishes around what proteins are available and what will complement them best.
Stocks: Broth made by "boiling bones with water," as Pépin puts it. It is the foundation for many, many sauces and seasonings.

Fast Food, Fast Career

It's a punch line that a useless college degree leads to a career in fast food. However, fast food and the growing market of "fast-casual" places can be great training grounds for prep work. It can also be a great place to start early on a career in the food industry. With hard work and focus, one can rise up fairly quickly. For example, the burrito chain Chipotle lists on its website the progression a full-time career can take, from starting in the kitchen crew to a restaurateur. A full-time worker in a corporate chain often has access

Don't look down on fast food. "Fast-casual" franchises are on the rise for people who want to eat something fresher than McDonald's but not much more expensive.

to benefits and possibly even tuition assistance of some sort. Although the US Bureau of Labor Statistics (BLS) puts the median pay of a fast-food worker lower than that of a prep or line cook, the BLS notes that this sector is still growing faster than the national job growth percentage in general, and specifically faster than the prep and line cooks positions.

Working up the ranks to the service manager level offers more than double the starting food service pay, and it can be achieved in the same amount of time it might take to go from dishwasher to line cook. So don't judge the fry cook at a McDonald's. Advancement comes quickly to those who pursue it and prove themselves worthy.

CHAPTER Two

Front of House

Cooks can be in the kitchen making all kinds of glorious dishes, but without a service staff to attend to the customers, the entrées will go uneaten. Wasting all that effort and food would be tragic, so thank goodness for the wait staff. The teams in the kitchen and in the dining room share the common goal of feeding the customers and giving them an experience worth paying for. Those who enjoy interacting with many different people will find the front of the house a natural outlet for their talents.

Welcome to ___________, I'll be Serving You Tonight

The variety of service roles increase as the size or elegance—or both—of the establishment also scales up. A Taco Bell might only have the cashier to ring up orders and an expeditor or counter server to hand over

Good service is as important as good food in a restaurant. Hard work and pleasant interactions are rewarded by customers in the form of tips.

orders when they're ready. A sit-down restaurant with a menu will have more serving personnel. The entry-level positions are organized to help the kitchen, the servers, or the bartender. These roles are known as busboys, food runners, or barbacks. These roles assist the servers who are the people interacting with the customers by taking their orders, explaining the menu, informing the kitchen of the pace of the meal, and fielding customer feedback. They are both salespeople and customer service representatives.

The table bussers keep the tables clean, the dining ware stocked, and sometimes run the orders out to the customers. Runners take food from the kitchen and deliver to the table. Arnold says the role can change depending on what kind of dining establishment it is, though, especially if it's a corporate chain compared to a privately owned place. "Corporate or chain locations follow a multitude of regulations, and they are uniform throughout. If you work at,

A waiter might take an order and bring it out, too. Other times, the waiter takes the order and a runner brings it out instead.

say, Chili's in Arkansas, you can find work at a Chili's in Washington. The rules and requirements are the same." In contrast, he goes on to say that, "Meanwhile, privately owned establishments will teach you a wide variety of skills, but some may not translate in other locations. As an expeditor at one location, I learned how to make salads, shuck oysters, build desserts, and pull espresso: all skills that make me more marketable, but never in the same field."

Sometimes, at a small place or a more casual one, the servers will also do the runner's or busser's job. However, there's still a uniform progression of career advancement overall: the runners/bussers to the servers to the maître d' or host/hostess to the general manager. The general manager is to the front of the house as the executive chef is to the kitchen, and these two restaurant heads generally will meet daily to discuss the menu, the staff available, the reservations in already from eager customers, and any other potential challenges they may need to face for a dining service. General managers are grouped under the Food Service Managers profile by the Bureau of Labor Statistics, which defines the role as "directing staff to ensure customers are satisfied with their dining experience." However, it's also their job to "manage the business to ensure that it is profitable." In other words, the general manager is in charge of the money, which is tracked in many ways. Does the menu accurately reflect both the price of the food ordered and the labor it took to cook it? Are enough customers coming in to cover not just everyone's paychecks, but also the rent of the restaurant's building or its mortgage and taxes? The

chef may decide what to order and where to order it from, but the general manager needs to set and approve the budget. If it seems like food is being wasted unnecessarily, that's a conversation for the general manager to have with the executive chef as well. There is no restaurant without a chef. But there's no long-lasting restaurant without a smart general manager keeping an eye on absolutely everything happening within it.

Tips for Better Tips

Someone who enjoys being social, talking to many different kinds of people and solving problems for them, can be very successful in the dining room. "Serving allows me to interact with people, which is where my talents lie," says Arnold. It can also be argued that the hours worked times the money made for a server is more profitable than for a cook.

Pay is more flexible depending on the tips a server

Being friendly and helpful—and patient—are useful skills for anyone working as service staff. Enjoying assisting people and solving their problems is a must.

can pick up. It's worth noting that Arnold works in a large entertainment establishment in the more touristy area of a major city. Still, it's true that the immediate benefit of waiting tables instead of cooking for them comes down to the tip left with the payment of the bill. The greater the satisfaction with the meal and service, hopefully, the bigger the tip. One can really make or break someone's dining experience. And the interactions can be a great way to better learn how to speak with people and understand them.

Having an interest in people is a great asset in waiting tables, as is a good memory, ability to track certain details, and paying attention to customers' needs, like an empty water glass. Arnold says:

> Fine dining is all about the atmosphere and experience. From being seated to an immediately filled water glass, to returning from the lavatory and finding your napkin folded beside your plate. The proper way to showcase a wine for guest tasting. One of the more interesting [details] I learned was when clearing plates was to clear from the right, and to never clear a lady's plate unless another diner has finished.

Sometimes, though, the requests can become more complicated or something can happen that threatens to ruin the meal for everyone. At that time, a good server will need patience and a willingness to solve the problem. Being able to keep one's temper and hold one's tongue are musts for dealing with customers who insist on having their way with everything. Sometimes, they want menu substitutions or alterations. Sometimes, they have a dispute regarding the pricing or where they're seated.

TWO DOTS AND A DASH

Kitchens have their own language when it comes to placing orders and keeping everyone organized. But the mid-twentieth-century diners are famous for having a specific kind of shorthand language when it came for the wait staff to relay the orders to the cooks. For example, a server might say to the counterman—someone who serves at the counter, as in a diner—"Get me some dirty water, and make it moo!" which meant a customer ordered a cup of coffee with milk. This lingo has faded out of usage, but it's still fun to think about what the kitchen staff all meant when they used these phrases. Take a look at the list below and try and figure out their meanings:

1. "Walk a cow though the garden and add yellow paint."
2. "That George Eddy ordered a battery acid and Adam and Eve on a raft."
3. "I need two dots and dash with a side of frog sticks!"
4. "Here's your hockey puck, hold the grass."
5. "Dessert on five, order of fish eyes!"

Answers:

A. A burger with lettuce, tomato, and onion, and add some mustard.

B. That customer didn't tip, after ordering a grapefruit juice and two poached eggs on toast.

(continued on the next page)

(continued from the previous page)

C. I need two fried eggs and strip of bacon with a side of French fries!
D. Here's your well-done burger, no lettuce.
E. Dessert on five, order of tapioca pudding!

Outside of an average difficult customer, sometimes the situation calls for support from the front of the house team. Management has the ability to offer concessions for any slights or issues. Free stuff, future reservations, etc. Perhaps a server forgot part of an order, and it arrived out of sequence, and the customers are upset. From there, a server can offer to put in as a rush, and if they still express dissatisfaction, one can offer to have the manager help with the situation. Never be afraid to ask the manager for help if a situation feels like it's getting out of hand. If it's obvious that you're doing your job to the fullest of your ability and the fault lies elsewhere, the manager is there to help.

The manager can work to appease a problem customer or she can draw a line and take action. "They are the line," says Arnold. "[One] guy refused to move his seat, insisted he didn't have to meet the table minimum, finally relented but ran me ragged over the first two hours, ignored me for the second, and stiffed me on the check," recounts Arnold. All of which was frustrating but manageable for Arnold to handle on his own. However, "had he continued to harass the staff, I had the manager on duty prepared to eject him."

Not all problems have to be frustrating with angry customers though. Arnold says:

> One instance was someone drinking something, and there was a bug in the ice. They called me over, calmly (thankfully) explained the situation, and said "we could discuss other concessions later." They got two rounds of drinks for four people, and still had a wonderful time, and tipped me handsomely for prompt response and good service.

What Arnold most appreciates about being in the front of the house is the sense of community with his customers. "Some people are there to eat, but some become your regulars. I have people who request me, regardless of my section, because we talk. I know them, their lives. There's a little old lady at my current job who always greets me with a big hug." Arnold laughs. "It's like I have several aunties and uncles...[who] all give me money like a holiday."

The One Who Knows All

For someone who's very detail-oriented and who likes to take charge of any situation, the role of the expeditor is extremely interesting. Expeditors work in the kitchen, but they're not the cooks. They need to keep track of all the orders, the timing, and the special requests, especially because they sometimes need to deal with upset customers. But they aren't the wait staff either. Instead, the expeditor is the liaison between the kitchen and the dining room. They tell the cooks what to make and when

The head chef or expeditor will work with the general manager to figure out the menu for the evening and how to handle the customers.

to have it ready. They also make sure that the runners grab the dishes as soon as they're plated. The job has been described as something similar to being an air traffic controller. There's a lot of information coming in all at once, which has to be processed immediately by the expeditor and redirected out to the correct parties after that. Sometimes, the head chef or sous-chef does expediting, but if one of them is out sick or just taking a day off, someone will still have to expedite the orders.

It is helpful to have culinary experience. In more high-end restaurants, the expeditor may be expected to help plate the dishes—that is, arrange the food in an attractive style on the plate or in the bowl from which the diner will be eating. Also, the expeditor may be required to quickly inspect and approve each dish before it can be served. If there's something wrong with the plate, it's good to be able to point exactly at the problem and tell the cook what specifically needs to be fixed.

Are there allergies or special considerations a customer has relayed to the wait staff? An expeditor not only needs to tell the cooks the correct information, but one also needs to be able to tell the server about the substations made or which dish is the special one among the others on the pass, the counter where cooked food waits to be brought out to the dining room. Is someone falling behind on his or her dishes? The expeditor can send someone over to help, like the *tournant*, the floating backup cook, or the expeditor can personally hop on the line to keep the kitchen moving. At the very least, the expeditor should alert the front of the house so that the general manager and wait staff can be proactive about how to handle any delays for the customers waiting to be fed.

A restaurant thrives on good, clear communication and teamwork. Kristina Francillon of the Genuine Kitchen blog compares expediting to being a conductor who orchestrates the stations behind the line in concert. No matter how well the cooks prepare the food and how well servers interact with their customers, they all need coordination, someone who can see who needs what when and who can give the right guidelines to keep everyone on track. Each role in a restaurant is connected to one another, and the chance to be that conductor can be extremely satisfying.

CHAPTER Three

Bringing the Food to You

Imagine going to a wedding and after the ceremony, the guests lifted glasses of tap water to the newlyweds and passed around a box of crackers to snack on. Imagine a cousin's Bar Mitzvah with only

Every special occasion is made better by sharing a meal. Caterers can help make a wedding or a celebration that much better through their skills.

the service, not the celebration afterward. There are any number of occasions that require food, but they may not be near a kitchen nor be able to be managed by the host personally. An office needs a special lunch for its employees. Who can they turn to who can make that happen? This looks like a job for the caterer!

Food That Travels

There's much about catering that resembles the challenges of restaurant cooking: the amount of prep, the need for timing and consistency, and the hierarchy. However, caterers often work within a set menu for the day as opposed to the larger à la carte menus of restaurants, which can have many, many dishes to prepare and coordinate. Often, wedding invitations ask guests to choose their entrées in advance, based on what the catering for the event has promised to provide. Whether it's a special celebration or a more corporate affair, catering is definitely an industry geared toward those who can afford it, which can make the paycheck more attractive.

The BLS places caterers in the category of food service managers, which can be seen as an indicator of somewhat better money. But their actual duties are a combination of the food service manager's role and the executive chef's role in the kitchen. The starting role is still prep cook, but in a smaller, more flexible kitchen like a catering business might have, there's certainly the chance of being more involved on the line sooner than one might in a restaurant kitchen. Zach Benson found himself taken into a five-person catering business more or less cold, with only a little experience several years prior in short-order and fast-

Like a restaurant kitchen, a catering kitchen needs a lot of prep work in order to succeed. A limited menu means larger quantities of fewer ingredients.

casual places. "I was really down on my luck. I found the catering job and worked really hard for them," says Benson. Within three years, his hard work had earned him the "second-in-command" spot before he moved on to the next stage of his career.

There are caterers who specialize in weddings and similar special occasions only, which can call for more advanced cooking. There are caterers who specialize in corporate catering, which can be mainly variations on sandwiches and salads. Caterers must work in kitchens officially licensed and approved by their state standards for commercial kitchens. They may have to obtain a variety of personal licenses and permits including things like a liquor license, normally the province of an entire restaurant's operation.

Catering to Their Every Need

The fundamental difference between a caterer and a restaurant is the approach to menus and their prep. Restaurants will have more variety in the ingredients being readied for service, but smaller amounts of them have to be prepped. In contrast, a catering company will have a set menu that nearly everyone will be eating all together, so the variety is restricted and the amounts to physically prep are greater. Benson refers to this as "batch cooking." At the beginning of the day when a chef arrives at work, there is a kind of a packet or a list of the things that must be prepared. There will also be a deadline for when the food needs to get out. Generally, caterers will have a heavier prep load because they are serving a large number of people with one dish.

The approach to cooking is also different. A restaurant prep list contains smaller amounts, but then each dish is being cooked to order. Cooks have to follow tickets as they come in, which makes the service unpredictable. More than that, a restaurant kitchen is at one set venue with presumably all the equipment the cooks will need for service each day. Caterers, however, must rely on portable sources of heat and refrigeration, especially if it's a venue without a kitchen. A fancy garden party is delightful for the guests, but the caterers may find themselves in an outdoor space, with no electricity or storage. They may also be subject to the whims of the weather. What a caterer can

An elaborate wedding depends on a smart caterer who keeps track of all the details needed to pamper guests on a couple's special day.

accomplish under challenging conditions depends partly on the menu put together and the mountain of prep work finished before even heading over to the venue.

THE HISTORY OF CATERING

According to the catering site Thank God It's Sofia, the term "catering" as it is used nowadays came out of the Merchant Marines. A special corps of officers known as catering officers had the duties assigned to them of procuring and preparing the food and then serving it to the others on board their ships.

That's the modern origin of the title and responsibilities. However, the concept of hiring teams of people to cook and serve the rich, the military, and those who could afford feasts is one rooted in ancient history. Evidence suggests that the idea of catering was around in China as far back as the fourth millennium BCE. More evidence indicates that the Greek and Roman empires had similar traditions of catered feasts, and so on up through medieval Europe. Caterers were available to feed travelers like crusading soldiers and religious pilgrims.

It was the rise of a comfortable middle class that led breweries and other food providers to start putting all kinds of restrictions on entertainment feasting. Ironically, these chefs moved into permanent venues and a new line of food service—the early restaurants.

What's useful in catering? Creativity and an understanding of what dishes can be done to fit the occasion and which ones to leave off. It may be expected to have a dessert for an event, for instance, would a meringue be a good choice? Probably not. It's too delicate and fussy for mass transportation and long periods of sitting out with no guarantee of its ideal storage temperature. In contrast, a brownie is sturdy and can be used in a variety of external conditions.

Instead of working with a front-of-the-house team, caterers may also have to be flexible about who will be serving the food to guests. Even if it's a buffet line where guests can serve themselves, someone should be available to explain the dishes, assist guests with service, and keep an eye on the amount of the food supply. Corporate and entertainment venues often will have their own event management teams who can coordinate with the catering personnel and provide them with servers. There are temporary placement services for cater-waiters, who are hired on an hourly basis for each event. However, in a pinch, the catering staff may find itself needing to serve the public directly. In those instances, one needs to be prepared to deal with many kinds of people and remain polite and helpful. For someone eager to come out from behind the stove occasionally, a career in catering is something worth considering. A caterer needs to be something of a salesperson and also be a self-starter who proactively finds new business. It's not a matter of being in one physical location and opening the doors to let new customers come in. Catering is about constantly hustling up new opportunities, which can be an exhilarating part of the job.

Catering needs people who are willing to coordinate with one another and the client in order to perfect every detail and create a special experience.

Catering is also about careful planning ahead of time. Once a catering team leaves the prep kitchen, everything is locked into place. So any special accommodations definitely need to be worked out in advance with the client. What can be done for a wedding where the groom has requested no tomatoes, onions, or garlic anywhere in the food, and the bride is a vegetarian? Each event is its own puzzle to be solved.

When Benson started catering, he found a significant advantage to catering cooking as opposed to restaurant cooking. Restaurant cooking is about each chef cooking part of a dish and putting them altogether at the same time on the same plate. “When [I] have a long line of tickets and [I’m] trying to fire everyone’s food to coincide with the other tickets that are being cooked by other people in the kitchen, I normally get pretty lost,” says Benson. “I think I personally am just better at catering or large-batch cooking because I have more control over my day and it’s easier for me to see the big picture.” The menus that may seem restrictive to the diners can be a blessing for the catering cooks who make the food. The ability to stay focused and plow through one’s “inbox,” as Arnold calls it, is something any cook finds useful.

CHAPTER Four

Home Is Where the Stove Is

For those who don't like the chaos and potential unpredictability of a restaurant kitchen—especially the hours—but who also want one steady location at which to report daily, there are other options out

Aspiring cooks and students who just need some money can find great opportunities on every university campus. Wherever there are people, there is a need for food.

there. A whole class of steadily employed, somewhat better paid, and stable kitchens exist outside of the restaurant industry. These aren't the glitzy kitchens or ones that explode into fine dining empires or fast-growing, fast-casual chains. Instead, they are the invaluable kitchens of the tourism industry, or perhaps they are the dining hubs of communal living spaces like college campuses and assisted-living facilities. Wherever there are large groups of people expecting to stay overnight for at least one day, there will be a kitchen. And that kitchen will need cooks.

Hotels and Tourist Attractions

There's a trend happening in very high-end hotels with fancy restaurants joining their operations. This is especially true in Las Vegas, where names like Wolfgang Puck and Bobby Flay are just as much tourist attractions as Celine Dion. But a Hilton, Marriott, or similar chain will have its own kitchen, too, with dining hours and room service attached to them. JobMonkey stresses that there can be many factors playing into the kitchen's schedule, but the number-one concern should be efficiency. People staying in a hotel are rarely doing so specifically to be at a hotel—unless it's one of those places like in Vegas with the casinos built in—so ensuring their dining needs are attended to as quickly as possible is the most important priority.

The hotel kitchen can find itself overlapping with a caterer's needs, if there's an event happening, like a reunion or a corporate retreat. A hotel might have a restaurant attached to it, but the menu is generally pretty fixed, which makes the prep work closer to the batch cooking style used by caterers and institutions. There may be a buffet. There may be room service. But the complicated assembly of dishes found in restaurants is a lower priority, generally speaking.

There can be professional rivalries between restaurant cooks and hotel ones, but there isn't any reason for it. Restaurants are where the press will shower its attention, but it's more volatile and less well paid than hotel cooking, so it's a false distinction. The Auguste Escoffier School of Culinary Arts is named after the father of modern French restaurants and dining as it was taught for decades. Auguste Escoffier introduced the method of organization

MEALS ON WHEELS

In March 2012, food writer Jonathan Gold wrote about the dazzling rise of the food truck. The United States was still harboring memories of the real estate crash in 2008 and looking for comfort food over fine dining, cheap over costly. But with the sophisticated palates of gourmets, what kind of food could entice them?

The food truck business has been a great way for underrepresented cuisines to find a public eager to experience them, and a less risky enterprise than opening a full-blown sit-down restaurant. Roy Choi is credited as the king of this revolution with his Korean barbecue truck that has become an empire. A food truck is a small, small venue to cook in and can only fit two to three people at most, but it gives each cook a degree of creativity and freedom he or she might not experience in a larger operation.

A food truck operation requires licenses and permits, but it allows the operation to find its most favorable venue. If one location doesn't work out, it's easy to pick up stakes—and steaks—and find a neighborhood that's ready for a whole new menu.

Food trucks are no longer just a craze; they're a way for people to get affordable, fresh food and for new business owners to get started.

the kitchens still practice today as far as the ranks and hierarchy go, and his recipes were deemed the standard for many years. Without Escoffier's influence, restaurants wouldn't have the impact on dining across many countries. And yet, this school promotes career paths for any kind of cook, not just restaurant ones. For those who want to truly use their skills to work anywhere, the travel chef has a career path laid out as well. Traveling to resorts or on cruise ships can mean the opportunity to see parts of the world one wouldn't otherwise be able to afford to go to.

In addition to the usual cooking and social skills one needs to have in any kitchen, a traveling chef will need a personal set of cook's tools. A small paring knife and a medium-size chef's

Many cruise lines have found success in advertising the luxurious dining experiences they've created for their passengers. People like to discover new places and cuisines.

knife will be the most important tools. Chef Cameron Stauch also recommends a travel spice kit, a cutting board, and measuring spoons and cups if possible. But the knives are the two most important things outside of the other key necessity: a current passport. It can take up to six weeks to get a passport request processed, so anyone planning on trying the life of a travel chef should get one requested before even answering a want ad for a cruise ship or a ski resort in the Alps.

A Home Away from Home

For those who don't live on their own for a variety of reasons—college dormitories, hospitals, assisted-living facilities—there's a benefit in having someone handle the food accommodations. Benson leveraged his catering work into four years working on a college campus and then took himself from Colorado to Oregon with a

Many elder care facilities have embraced quality eating experiences for their residents, including tastier dishes and fresher ingredients.

job at an assisted-living facility, confident that wherever he wanted to go, his experience now qualified him for work anywhere. Although he started at the bottom of the kitchen chain at the college job, he approached it with confidence.

Cooks working in the kitchens of assisted living centers might find that the pay is better and there is plenty of kitchen help because these kinds of places have more money to spend on food service. There isn't one person's business on the line day in and day out, which can add a lot of stress to the kitchen. The money also helps the kitchen itself run more smoothly. If equipment breaks, it can fixed or replaced more quickly.

There are still differences from kitchen to kitchen though, including in personnel. A college campus will have a lot of students in the kitchens alongside the permanent crews as a way to help students with their financial aid needs. Although a kitchen should always be keeping an eye on the budget, especially with thousands of potential diners who need feeding, Benson does see a considerable difference from his college kitchen work to his current position. "The quality of food we worked with was not that great. I do large-batch cooking at this assisted-living home now, and we butcher our meat and shred and cut all our vegetables and fruits instead of buying anything premade or cut to keep costs down opposed to the campus, which would just buy lower-quality products to save money." Benson is hopeful that change is coming to his former place of employment. Large-batch cooking doesn't have to be awful food, is Benson's feeling. He found himself fortunate to work in two responsible kitchens, which operated under budget for food costs. This means for kitchens who want to grow

There are a lot of processed ingredients in batch-cooking kitchens, but there's also support for the teams and their environments.

in quality, there are ways to achieve that without being too expensive to run.

Still, although Benson has found himself a comfortable life in nonrestaurant kitchens, he sees his eventual career turning back to them as he progresses as a leader. "I would like to be in a leadership position at a bare minimum, and I feel I am on that path, My absolute dream would be a place, which would be like [my first restaurant job] except with a way better sound system and all our sandwich stuff would be made from scratch." Benson's first love was music, and his aspiration could allow him to combine his passion and career into one ideal goal.

CHAPTER *Five*

What You Need to Succeed

In case it hasn't already been made clear, the restaurant business is hard, hard work. Physically, there's the stress of a hot kitchen, standing for hours and hours—or running back and forth for hours and hours—and performing the same task over and over.

Cooking professionally does require an ability to endure tough working conditions and equally tough schedules. Remaining healthy can be very helpful for one's job performance.

Mentally, there are details to track, focus to maintain, and criticism to accept. There can be a lot of satisfaction in a job well done at the end of every shift, but any older, more experienced chef will still issue warnings that the life is harder than one might expect.

A Tough Body and a Strong Stomach

Think of the squats one does at the gym. Up and down, pushing oneself back up repeatedly, or doing lunges across the floor for several reps. It's exhausting work, and it builds a strong set of muscles. But that's also voluntary work. At a kitchen, a cook will have to bend over a stove, crouch down to the ground to retrieve ingredients from the low-boy, the storage unit underneath the station, and then spring back up in order to keep the dish moving. And this is something one will have to do every workday for hours and hours because space in a kitchen is limited, so one can only take out what one needs each time. The late Anthony Bourdain was publicly thankful more than once that his

Professional kitchens of all kinds require a lot of bending down, lifting, running around, and handling of hot stoves and sharp knives.

writing career took off just when he was hitting middle age and his knees were starting to go bad.

The kitchen is full of hot flames, sharp knives, and blasts of steam, usually in a very small space for the amount of people who have to move through it for eight to ten hours at a time. Bill Buford wrote in his book *Heat: An Amateur's Adventures as Kitchen Slave, Line Cook, Pasta-Maker, and Apprentice to a Dante-Quoting Butcher in Tuscany* about taking over the grill during a very hot summer. Although his kitchen was air-conditioned in general, it wasn't at all chilled at his station because the heat needed to stay consistent. He came off his shift completely dehydrated. Spend a Fourth of July afternoon outside on a grill for a family occasion, and that may help give an idea of the heat one endures in the kitchen, though it probably won't come with the speed or barrage of information on top of it.

Coworkers can either be a strong community for the cooks, or they can be problematic if a clique forms and leaves a person out. Some cooks find that the kitchen is a good place for introverts. A chef can be be pretty antisocial in a kitchen, but at the same time work toward building relationships with other staff members.

Any time spent cleaning out a home refrigerator can be full of unpleasant discoveries. Yogurts gone unfinished and shoved to the back of the fridge along with leftovers from six months ago, or vegetables bought in a burst of good intentions sitting around in the crisper all go rotten sooner than expected. A restaurant has to stay on top of its food's freshness very vigilantly. Its reputation and legal standing are at risk if anyone gets food poisoning from ingredients that lingered too long at the back of the walk-in cooler. It's the kitchen staff who have to inspect every item prepped for service, and sometimes, there are unpleasant surprises.

What happens with food that a diner doesn't want? There's trash constantly piling up, and where there's trash, there's vermin. A constant battle has to be waged against mice, rats, and cockroaches. A person who has trouble dealing with bugs and rodents needs to be aware that the kitchen is a good place for such creatures to be hiding out and that they have to be eliminated whenever they make an appearance. The fear that a diner may come face to snout with a mouse is real and needs never to happen. Do not let the animals run the zoo.

Health inspections help a restaurant adhere to standards in order to prevent spoiled food, cross-contamination from raw ingredients, and the presence of vermin. According to the site WebstaurantStore, health codes vary from state to state. The Food and Drug Administration (FDA), which first standardized the food code from which all local ones are derived, monitors all health codes and the companies that enforce them. A clean bill of inspection or a high score doesn't mean the restaurant is completely sterilized. It only means that the levels of vigilance have been strong enough to keep the low-risk violations to a minimum. Every day, there are bags and bags of garbage piling up, meat to be butchered, fish to be cleaned, and leftover ingredients to be inspected. Someone who's easily nauseated by strong smells and slimy textures will find a professional kitchen difficult to work in.

A Professional Attitude

Working in a restaurant is often compared to the military, right down to the pots and pans, which are sometimes known as the *batterie de cuisine*, the artillery of the

ALL THE WORLD'S A STAGE

For those who are truly committed to learning about high-end cuisine and who want to learn the best techniques, it's common in the food world to go on *stages* (pronounced stah-jes), which are unpaid internships. It can be an excellent way to bolster a résumé. To *stage* is generally to work in a place outside of the United States, although a stint at a restaurant like the French Laundry in Yountville, California, is certainly on par with any fancy place in France.

Although *stages* may seem like a great way to take advantage of eager labor, even well-established cooks will take the time to go travel and learn from new mentors. It's the best way to develop new skills and be exposed to new cuisines. Despite the lack of pay, these spots can be very competitive and can hold the potential to elevate a career in the future.

However, the most important part of a *stage* is simply getting to eat! Even if one can't travel abroad, it's good to take that lesson of learning and apply it locally. In other words—eat! Try everything!

kitchen. New additions to the kitchen are expected to take a lot of orders and execute them without complaint or backtalk. Therefore, during the interview process a job candidate needs to communicate the ability to be cooperative and eager to learn.

In any job search, there will be classified ads in the local paper or online through industry forums. Restaurants might also hang a "now hiring" sign right in the window when they need new people. Benson got his start through friends and family telling him where to apply because they had an inside track with the bosses, but his big catering break came from following up on a classified ad on the internet. Arnold started his career young, right in the dish pit through the local resources in his town. "I got that gig from the local classified section, at fourteen." There weren't a lot of opportunities for someone needing to work that young, and he was happy to have found a place that was hiring.

Libraries can be great places for free newspapers and internet access in order to hunt down a job ad. But also hanging around a favorite restaurant and getting to know the staff there can be useful. Even if they don't have an opening, the community and network of kitchen professionals is strong, and they can steer a new applicant to a position not yet widely advertised.

A person in search of employment should always wear clean clothes that are on the conservative side of style. Even if this is a first job and no résumé can be put together yet, thinking of examples in which the applicant has helped out around the house, in the greater community, or at school may give an idea to the hiring manager whether the applicant is capable of taking orders, learning quickly, and showing up on time every shift.

Resources for job hunting can be found at libraries and community job centers. Every job interview requires clean, neat clothing and a good attitude.

When it comes to interviews, aim to keep answers concise and related to the position under discussion. A question like "tell me about yourself" does not mean tell one's whole life story. Instead, keep it to the present including what job level you have in mind—like permanent or part-time—how you found out about the job, and why that one specifically interests you. Be honest but polite. Everyone needs a job for money. Think about why you can be an asset to the kitchen as opposed to how the kitchen will benefit you. If you are asked if you know how to do something, be honest if you don't know it right now. A restaurant can teach anyone willing to learn, but they should know exactly where to start with the training. Benson says, "If you show up on time every day, don't abuse breaks, and are always willing to do whatever is asked of you, there is always a kitchen to work in."

Ready to Get Schooled?

The debate on whether culinary schools or on-the-job training helps a professional cook the most is never-ending. There are vocational schools that can teach basic cooking skills, but to someone like Jacques Pépin, who came up through the rigorous training of the professional French kitchen, there's no substitute for hard work done over and over again. "A great chef is first a great technician," he says. "You have no choice as a professional chef; you have to repeat, repeat, repeat, repeat until it becomes part of yourself." And culinary schools, such as the prestigious Culinary Institute of America (CIA), can give eager students the opportunity to experiment and train to become efficient and professional cooking machines. But will they give much advantage out in the real hiring world? Anthony Bourdain spoke fondly of the kitchen as the "last meritocracy," where technique and ability are earned through hard work, day in and day out. Although a graduate of CIA himself, Bourdain put more stock in the hard workers who came into the kitchen young and rose up through the ranks then he did any graduate of a culinary college.

Eater dedicated a long feature to this conversation and found many supporters of the schooling environment as the training ground. Schools can give a safe and supportive environment to work up the skills and speed necessary to be successful in the kitchen. But the BLS notes in both the prep workers sections and the line cooks entry that prior experience isn't necessary. Formal, on-the-job training is expected instead. Schools can be great for building up skills, for exploring all kinds of cuisines and techniques outside of one kitchen's style only, and for building up a strong network. A completed degree demonstrates to future employers the dedication to see hard work through to the end and guarantees a certain level of skill. But the price of a degree

Chefs keep debating the need for culinary schools. Some make a career without one and learn on the job. Others find the networking opportunities especially helpful.

can be on par with the cost of a college degree in a liberal arts field, and the starting pay for a new applicant just walking in the door is the same, regardless of education or not. One has to weigh whether the potential advantages of earning a culinary degree will move a cooking career along more quickly than going in full-time without a degree. At the end of the day, it's the cook's own abilities that matter the most, no matter how he or she has learned.

Glossary

À LA CARTE This refers to the menu and used to literally mean a piece of paper. To order à la carte is to order whatever individual dishes from the menu as the customer pleases.

BATCH COOKING Prepping and cooking up a huge amount of ingredients for a limited menu.

BATTERIE DE CUISINE Literally, this translates to "the artillery of the kitchen" and refers to the pots and pans a kitchen uses in its cooking.

CHEF'S KNIFE A basic, all-purpose knife that can be used from the delicate mincing of garlic all the way up to carving through cuts of meat.

COMPONENT A particular part of any one dish. Components are assembled together on one plate or bowl during the plating process.

DISH PIT The part of the kitchen dedicated to the dishwashers as they scrape and clean plates and wash every single dish used for dining or cooking.

EXECUTIVE CHEF The head chef in the kitchen, who usually plans the menu and orders the food.

EXPEDITOR The liaison between the kitchen and the dining room, who's in charge of relaying orders to the cooks and completed dishes to the servers.

FOOD CODE The model regulations set by the US Food and Drug Administration by which state and local health departments create their health codes for restaurants.

FRONT OF HOUSE The staff who interact directly with the customers in the dining room of a restaurant.

"IN THE WEEDS" A phrase used to describe falling behind one's duties during service; a cook in the weeds risks slowing the whole kitchen down.

MISE-EN-PLACE A French phrase meaning "everything in place." In the kitchen, it refers to all the ingredients and tools a cook needs at his or her station for the shift's service.

PARING KNIFE A small knife most often used to peel fruits and vegetables.

PLATING The arrangement of the components of a dish. This is done in a deliberate manner, intended to create the most appetizing look for the entrée as well as keeping the components in their tastiest conditions.

PROTEIN The component that's usually the star of a dish. This can be the meat from an animal, like a cow or a duck, or from seafood, like lobsters, or even from beans and nuts, like tofu or pine nuts in pesto.

SAUCE To pour or smear the sauce component of the dish onto the plate and components.

SERVER The employee running completed dishes from the kitchen to their customers in the dining room.

SERVICE The time during which a restaurant is open to feed customers.

SHIFT The amount of time a worker is expected to be in the kitchen, often much longer than the service itself runs.

SOUS-CHEF The second-in-command chef under the executive chef.

TASTING MENU A special menu in fine dining establishments, where multiple courses of very small portions are prepared for a table of guests.

TECHNIQUE The ability to execute a method of cooking with a particular tool or set of tools. Good cooking relies on the knowledge and mastery of good techniques.

"THE LINE" The stations where the cooks are preparing the food for the diners. A line cook is someone who is directly cooking for customers.

"THE PASS" The shelf or counter where completed dishes sit when they're ready to be picked up by the server and delivered to diners.

For More Information

Auguste Escoffier School of Culinary Arts
637 S. Broadway H
Boulder, CO 80305
(877) 249-0305
Website: https://www.escoffier.edu
Facebook and Twitter: @escoffierschool
The culinary school named after the father of French restaurants has two campuses, one in Colorado and one in Texas, as well as an online campus.

Canada's Food Guide
Health Canada
Address Locator 0900C2
Ottawa, Ontario K1A 0K9
Canada
(613) 957-2991
Website: https://www.canada.ca/en/health-canada/services/food-nutrition/canada-food-guide/using-food-guide.html
The Canadian government supplies this resource for making "wise food choices" in one's diet, regardless of where one is eating.

Choose Restaurants
2055 L Street NW
Washington, DC 20036
(800) 424-5156
Website: https://chooserestaurants.org
Facebook: @NRAEFoundation
Twitter: @NRAEF
Instagram: @prostartprogram
The educational arm of the National Restaurant

Association is especially helpful for aspiring young culinary candidates.

Culinary Academy of Las Vegas
710 West Lake Mead Boulevard
North Las Vegas, NV 89030
(702) 924-2100
Website: http://www.theculinaryacademy.org
Facebook and Twitter: @CulinaryLV
Instagram: @culinaryacademylv
The Culinary Academy of Las Vegas is specifically devoted to reducing unemployment and poverty by giving its students the vocational skills and learning required for a life on the cooking line.

Culinary Institute of America (CIA)
1946 Campus Drive
Hyde Park, NY 12538
(845) 452-9600
Website: https://www.ciachef.edu
Facebook: @CIAchef
Twitter: @CIACulinary
The premier culinary school in the United States teaches students looking for the best cooking education.

Just Food
114 West 47th Street, Suite C1-35
New York, NY 10036
(212) 645-9880
Website: http://www.justfood.org
Facebook: @justfood.org
Twitter: @justfood

This nonprofit organization is devoted to food justice and sustainable community agriculture. It offers an excellent guide to learning about food issues in one's community.

Stratford Chefs School
192 Ontario Street
Stratford, Ontario N5A 3H4
Canada
(519) 271-1414
Website: https://stratfordchef.com
Facebook: @StratfordChefsSchool
Twitter: @StratfordChef
Instagram: @stratfordchefsschool
This Canadian culinary school emphasizes hands-on training and apprenticeships.

Young Workers Project
Labor Occupational Health Program
University of California at Berkeley
University Hall, Suite 451
2199 Addison Street, 4th Floor
Berkeley, California 94720-7360
Phone: (510) 642-5507
Fax: (510) 643-5698
Website: http://youngworkers.org
Facebook: @youngworkersCA
Twitter and Instagram: @youngworkers_CA
A resource dedicated to keeping young adult and teen workers safe on the job. The laws are specific to California, but it provides resources to get started on research for job safety regulations.

Youth Job Center
1114 Church Street
Evanston, IL 60201
Phone: (847) 864-5627
Fax: (847) 864-3098
Email: info@youthjobcenter.org
Website: http://youthjobcenter.org
Facebook: @yjcevanston
Twitter: @YouthJobCenter
The Youth Job Center has been helping teens find jobs for over thirty-five years for communities in Chicago, Evanston, and Cook County.

For Further Reading

Ayer, Paula. *Foodprints: The Story of What We Eat.* Toronto, ON: Annick Press, 2015.

Bayless, Rick, and Lanie Bayless. *Rick & Lanie's Excellent Kitchen Adventures: Chef-Dad, Teenage Daughter, Recipes, and Stories*. New York, NY: Stewart, Tabori and Chang, 2004.

Child, Julia, and David Nussbaum. *Julia's Kitchen Wisdom: Essential Techniques and Recipes from a Lifetime of Cooking*. 3rd. ed. New York, NY: Knopf, 2009.

Christen, Carol, and Richard N. Bolles. *What Color Is Your Parachute? for Teens.* 3rd ed. Emeryville, CA: Ten Speed Press, 2015.

Edwards, Jim. *Rookie Cooking: Every Great Cook Has to Start Somewhere.* New York, NY: Skyhorse Publishing, 2017.

Gibney, Michael. *Sous Chef: 24 Hours on the Line*. New York, NY: Ballantine, 2015.

Gordon Reeves, Emily. *Can I Wear My Nose Ring to the Interview?: A Crash Course in Finding, Landing, and Keeping Your First Real Job*. New York, NY: Workman, 2009.

Hamilton, Gabrielle. *Blood, Bones & Butter: The Inadvertent Education of a Reluctant Chef*. New York, NY: Random House, 2012.

Hazen, Marcella. *Essentials of Classic Italian Cooking*. New York, NY: Knopf, 2012.

Heos, Bridget. *Urban Gardening and Farming for Teens: Jarring and Canning*. New York, NY: Rosen Publishing, 2014.

Hubbard, Rita. *Job Basics: Getting the Job You Need: Getting a Job in the Food Industry*. New York, NY:

Rosen Publishing, 2014.

Kallen, Stuart A. *Exploring Careers: Careers in Food and Agriculture*. San Diego, CA: ReferencePoint Press, 2018.

Kelley, Thea. *Get That Job!: The Quick and Complete Guide to a Winning Interview*. San Francisco, CA: Thea Kelley, 2012.

Lehman, Jeff. *First Job, First Paycheck: How to Get the Most Out of Both…Without Help from Your Parents*. Seattle, WA: Mentor Press LLC, 2011.

Lore, Nicholas. *Now What? The Young Person's Guide to Choosing the Perfect Career.* New York, NY: Touchstone, 2008.

Marin, Susannah. *Spice Mixes: 39 Spices And Herbs Mixes From Around The World That Every Chef Should Know*. North Charleston, SC: CreateSpace, 2015.

Meyer, Susan. *Essential Careers: A Career as a Chef*. New York, NY: Rosen Publishing, 2015.

Nosrat, Samin. *Salt, Fat, Acid, Heat: Mastering the Elements of Good Cooking*. 4th ed. New York, NY: Simon & Schuster, 2017.

Page, Karen, and Andrew Dornenburg. *The Flavor Bible: The Essential Guide to Culinary Creativity, Based on the Wisdom of America's Most Imaginative Chefs*. New York, NY: Little, Brown and Company, 2008.

Robins, Rebecca. *Small Potatoes: A Young Chef's Apprenticeship in 19th Century Paris*. Seattle, WA: Amazon Digital Services, 2013.

Smith, Remmi. *The Healthy Teen Cookbook: Around the World in 80 Fantastic Recipes*. Miami, FL: Mango Publishing, 2018.

Weiser, Katie. *Answers to the Top 20 Interview Questions: Conquering the Job Interview Process*. North Charleston, SC: CreateSpace, 2017.

Bibliography

Bourdain, Anthony. *Medium Raw*. New York, NY: Ecco, 2011.

Buford, Bill. *Heat*. New York, NY: Vintage, 2007.

Culinary Cook, The. "Interested in a Cooking Career? 8 Questions Chefs Ask Will Ask You." February 15, 2015. https://theculinarycook.com/8-questions-chefs-ask-cooking-career.

Escoffier.edu Blog. "Cooking Across the World: Life as a Travel Chef." August 12, 2016. https://www.escoffier.edu/blog/culinary-arts/cooking-across-the-world-life-as-a-travel-chef.

Fayed, Saad. "Cooking Terms and Techniques for Absolute Beginners." The Spruce, March 2, 2018. https://www.thespruceeats.com/beginner-cooking-terms-and-techniques-2356056.

Francillon, Kristina. "Expediting the Genuine Kitchen: A Method to the Madness." The Genuine Kitchen, August 25, 2014. https://thegenuinekitchen.com/2014/08/25/expediting-the-genuine-kitchen-a-method-to-the-madness.

Gold, Jonathan. "How America Became a Food Truck Nation." *Smithsonian Magazine*, March 2012. https://www.smithsonianmag.com/travel/how-america-became-a-food-truck-nation-99979799.

Gordinier, Jeff. "There's the Wrong Way and Jacques Pépin's Way." *New York Times*, October 18, 2011. https://nyti.ms/pj2Aqt.

Job Monkey. "Chef Jobs at Hotels." Retrieved March 2, 2018. http://www.jobmonkey.com/chefjobs/hotel-cooks.

Jordan Arnold, interviewed by Rachel Gluckstern. New York, NY, February 26, 2018.

Kamp, David. *The United States of Arugula: The Sun Dried, Cold Pressed, Dark Roasted, Extra Virgin Story of the American Food Revolution*. New York, NY: Broadway Books, 2006.

Learn.org. "What Are the Duties of a Restaurant General Manager?" Retrieved February 28, 2018. https://learn.org/articles/What_are_the_Duties_of_a_Restaurant_General_Manager.html.

Lienard, Sarah. "25 Skills Every Cook Should Know." BBC Good Food.com. Retrieved February 28, 2018. https://www.bbcgoodfood.com/howto/guide/25-skills-every-cook-should-know.

Mattox, Charlyne, and Chris Morocco. "6 Cooking Techniques Everyone Needs to Know." *Real Simple*. Retrieved February 28, 2018. https://www.realsimple.com/food-recipes/cooking-tips-techniques/cooking-techniques#macerated-red-onion.

McKeever, Amy. "Culinary School: the Pros and Cons of Culinary Education." Eater, July 11, 2013. https://www.eater.com/2013/7/11/6408893/culinary-school-the-pros-and-cons-of-culinary-education.

Pépin, Jacques. *Jacques Pépin New Complete Techniques*. New York, NY: Black Dog and Leventhal, 2012.

Society for Human Resource Management. "Restaurant Expeditor." Retrieved February 28, 2018. https://www.shrm.org/resourcesandtools/tools-and-samples/job-descriptions/pages/cms_006467.aspx.

Tuder, Stephanie. "Why You Should Become a Restaurant Expeditor." *Sirvo*. October 21, 2016. https://sirvo.com/career/become-restaurant-food-expeditor.

US Bureau of Labor Statistics. "Chefs and Head Cooks." Retrieved February 28, 2018. https://www.bls.gov/ooh/food-preparation-and-serving/chefs-and-head-cooks.htm.

US Bureau of Labor Statistics. "Cooks." Retrieved February 28, 2018. https://www.bls.gov/ooh/food-preparation-and-serving/cooks.htm.

US Bureau of Labor Statistics. "Food and Beverage Serving and Related Workers." Retrieved February 28, 2018. https://www.bls.gov/ooh/food-preparation-and-serving/food-and-beverage-serving-and-related-workers.htm.

US Bureau of Labor Statistics. "Food Preparation Workers." Retrieved February 28, 2018. https://www.bls.gov/ooh/food-preparation-and-serving/food-preparation-workers.htm.

US Bureau of Labor Statistics. "Food Service Managers." Retrieved February 28, 2018. https://www.bls.gov/ooh/management/food-service-managers.htm.

US Bureau of Labor Statistics. "Waiters and Waitresses." Retrieved February 28, 2018. https://www.bls.gov/ooh/food-preparation-and-serving/waiters-and-waitresses.htm.

WebstaurantStore. "Preparing for a Health Inspection." March 21, 2018. https://www.webstaurantstore.com/article/16/health-inspection-checklist.html.

Wong, Bettie. "How to Start a Catering Business." LegalZoom, January 2015. https://www.legalzoom.com/articles/how-to-start-a-catering-business.

Zach Benson, interviewed by Rachel Gluckstern. New York, NY, February 23, 2018.

Index